Mastering Your Process

Creating Habits That Lead to Successful

Outcomes

Christopher J. Robinson

Copyright © 2023 Christopher J. Robinson

ISBN: 979-8-218-13496-9

All rights reserved. No portion of this document may be reproduced in any form without expressed, written consent from the author. This book was self-published by the author with the help of BusyB Writing.

DEDICATION

I want to dedicate this book to my children, Chris Jr., Aalesia, Cameryn, and Brielle. Being your father has provided me with more lessons and blessings than any other source. The principles within this book come from my passion for enlightening others on ways to better improve their lives. I hope I continue to do my job as your father—giving you access to knowledge and wisdom that will serve you throughout your lives.

CONTENTS

DEDICATION 3

INTRODUCTION 9

WHY ARE WE SO OUTCOME-DRIVEN? 12

BENEFITS | BEING OUTCOME-DRIVEN 20

UNINTENDED CONSEQUENCES OF BEING OUTCOME-DRIVEN 32

BECOMING PROCESS-DRIVEN 42

BENEFITS | BEING PROCESS-DRIVEN 51

USING OUTCOMES TO ESTABLISH YOUR PROCESS 61

PEOPLE SUCCESSFULLY MASTERING THEIR PROCESS 69

ESTABLISHING YOUR PROCESS (ACTION PLAN) 108

CONCLUSION 123

ACKNOWLEDGMENTS 127

Mastering Your Process

INTRODUCTION

If you are reading this book, you have likely decided to learn strategies to increase your level of success regarding your personal goals. Your goal may be to save more money, get in better shape, improve a relationship, achieve a new status within your career, or accomplish something else that's important to you. Regardless of what brought you to this book, you are here now, and you're already taking steps to increase your chances at successful outcomes.

This book is for anyone who wants to create habits that will result in them reaching the outcomes in their lives that they desire. Most successful people can relate to the importance of always having goals to focus on. The objective might be building a new business and breaking down all the steps on how to get that business to be successful. Or it may be an athlete who has a strict regimen on how they eat, exercise, train, and review video footage of their games. Regardless, those who are most successful usually outline the steps that they need to follow, remain disciplined in following those steps, and are purposeful in working toward their goals. At some point or another, most will succeed in achieving goals this way. Maybe you are someone who outlined steps they needed to take to make the soccer team, or maybe you are someone who wanted to lose a certain amount of weight before your wedding. In either case, to be successful, you likely outlined concise steps that would lead to your goal and then put the effort in to achieve it.

Although this is how most of us view success and visualize goals, there are some gaps in this line of thinking that prevent us from reaching our highest potential. This is a very outcome-driven way of looking at achievement. In this book, we will outline the benefits of this perspective as well as the benefits of being more process-driven.

Imagine that you could shift the way you see your goals, increase your overall potential, *and* gain benefits that you didn't even expect. It's like going to work for a week without having an agreed-upon amount of money that you were supposed to earn and ultimately earning twice as much due to your efforts. That's how being process-driven feels.

Over the last 10 years of providing therapy to clients, one of the strategies that has rendered the greatest results is shifting the way they see their goals. In therapy, clients are driven to improve some aspect(s) of their lives, such as their work-life balance, anger management, marriage, parenting skills, anxiety, or some other important area. So, when starting therapy, you always begin with a complete assessment of where the client is and what they want to accomplish. This leads to their treatment plan, which contains their goals and objectives. With this, they have some idea of where they are going and what they are trying to achieve. By helping clients become more process driven and focused on their habits, they can accomplish their original goals *and* improve in many other areas of their lives that they didn't even consider.

The principles we discuss in this book can also be applied to groups, teams, families, couples, and partnerships alike. In the coming chapters, we will outline the different ways people see their goals as well as the benefits of shifting to a more process-driven mindset.

CHAPTER 1: WHY ARE WE SO OUTCOME-DRIVEN?

What does it mean to be outcome-driven? More specifically, what would be an outcome-driven goal? This is a question that is usually easy for someone to answer. For the sake of being on the same page, we will define outcome-driven as being focused on an outcome. Regarding a goal, this mindset highlights what will occur at the end of our efforts. A very easy example would be if I said I wanted to lose five pounds in one month. That would mean at the end of the month, I should be five pounds less than what I am now. So, losing five pounds would be the outcome, and I am driven to achieve that outcome with my actions.

Starting in our earliest developmental years, we learn to be outcome-driven. This mindset has a lot of benefits and creates a way for us to stay focused on trying to achieve what we deem important. Think about it. Back in your early days in school, what was most important to you?

Christopher Robinson

For many of us, it was our grades because that was a way to demonstrate that we were gaining a level of competency regarding what was being taught. As students, earning good grades was a way to make us feel good about showing what we knew.

I can remember way back when I would get a spelling test that said "100%" or "A+!" Grades like that were so good that my teacher would put the tests on the wall to show everyone in the class that those students were special. Thinking back on getting those A+s and what it took to achieve them is key to understanding the outcome-driven mindset.

You first set the goal of getting 100%. Then, you had to have a way to make sure that you'd be able to spell every word correctly when you took the spelling test. There were many ways to do this. You could take time at home and study your spelling words by yourself. You could work in groups with other classmates to test each other on the words. You could write the words down over and over until their spellings were stuck in your memory. Or you could even sit next to a classmate you knew could spell well and see if you could get a glimpse of their test while taking your test (cheating).

Mastering Your Process

At this level of thinking, *how* you achieved the goal of getting an A+ meant very little. As long as the teacher gave you your test back and it said "100%," you felt successful. This way of thinking is reinforced time and time again as we age. "By any means necessary" is one of the most common phrases you'll hear people say when speaking about an outcome that is important to them. This is a saying many remember from Malcolm X. By using this phrase, he insinuated that he would get his desired outcome no matter what tactics were required of him and his people.

Basically, saying, "By any means necessary," means you don't care *how* you achieve your goal because you'll make sure you achieve it no matter what you must do. This creates a mindset that you cannot be stopped when it comes to your goals. There are a lot of benefits to thinking this way, and it can create a high level of motivation to continue pursuing your goal, even if things get difficult or tricky.

Pop culture has also reinforced the concept of being outcome-driven with little focus on the how. One example of this is the title of a very popular rap album by 50 Cent called *Get Rich or Die Tryin'*. According to Wikipedia, in 2020, it was certified nine-times platinum by the Recording Industry Association of America (RIAA). In the U.S., it was the best-selling album of 2003, and it was nominated for Best Rap Album at the 46th Grammy Awards. It also won Favorite Rap/Hip-Hop Album at the 2003 American Music Awards and was a Top Billboard 200 Album at the 2003 Billboard Music Awards. In 2020, Rolling Stone even ranked the album #280 on their updated 500 Greatest Albums of All Time list.

When looking at the title of this famous album, it is easy to see the outcome 50 Cent is trying to achieve. He is obviously highly focused on getting rich. This is something that many aspire to be, especially those who come from humble beginnings. The thing that I want you to focus on is *how* 50 is trying to get rich. He does not explicitly state this, but he highlights that he will do whatever it takes, even if it leads to him dying. Very few people want to die, so having that willingness to achieve an outcome means the outcome is more important than the how.

Now, let's look at how 50 got rich. Some would just say he became a famous rapper, but if you look deeper into his early life, you can see his journey to getting rich. In his drugs-to-riches memoir, *From Pieces*

Mastering Your Process to Weight: Once Upon a Time in Southside Queens, he says, "Nothing I was being told in school made sense to my reality...I could break down a kilogram of cocaine into ounces, grams, or any combination of the two. That's how I learned my fractions and metric conversion, through real-life applications."

At that point, 50 had made his mind up that the way for him to get rich would be to sell drugs. Even when he began to rap for a career, his music was about drugs, the world that comes with them, and the people he interacted with. Later, we will discuss one of his early songs, "Ghetto Quran."

Another great example of focusing on the outcome of getting rich is the story of Bernie Madoff. At the height of Bernie's success, he was estimated to be worth billions of dollars. When breaking down the "how" of his earning his wealth, you must go back to the 60s, when he began his Wall Street career as a trader. This led to him forming his business, Bernard L. Madoff Investment Securities LLC, and eventually occupying prominent positions in the industry's organizations, such as Chairman of NASDAQ Exchange and Chairman of the Board of Directors of the National Association of Securities Dealers (NASD).

Bernie used his experience and reputation to gain the trust of very wealthy and powerful people on Wall Street. He then used that trust to secure billions of dollars from investors, promising extraordinarily high returns on their investments. This was the premise of one of—if not the most—famous Ponzi schemes in history. Simply put, Bernie would take large sums of money from investors, falsify documentation showing that their money was earning interest, and pay early investors with money that was collected from the new investor—never investing the actual money of any investor.

When evaluating this situation with an outcome-driven mindset, one would say that Bernie was widely successful. If the goal was to be rich beyond your imaginable dreams, he obviously achieved that by gaining access to billions of dollars. According to *The Economic Times*, "In 2009, Court documents show[ed] that Bernard Madoff and his wife Ruth lived a life of high luxury, with exclusive homes, yachts, and other assets worth $823 million."

At this point, you're probably thinking, "What's wrong with being outcome-driven?" Most of us have been conditioned to be outcome-driven, and those who are most successful are usually good at setting and attaining goals with this kind of mindset. So, what other things should you consider outside of the outcome? This book is not an outline to discredit outcome-driven people. Being outcome-driven is a paramount principle in having a successful life for most of us, myself included. In the next chapter, we will highlight some of the benefits of outcome-driven goals and start to highlight other things we should consider when moving in a direction to attain the things that are most important to us.

CHAPTER 1 KEY POINTS:

- We are conditioned at an early age to be outcome-driven. This is reinforced through examples of successful individuals and media.

- The outcome of a goal is usually emphasized more than how you achieve the goal. The quote by Malcolm X, "By any means necessary," is an example of this.

CHAPTER 2: THE BENEFITS OF BEING OUTCOME-DRIVEN

To better explore the benefits of being outcome-driven, I think it's important to explain the aspects of a well-written goal. To do that, we will use the SMART acronym to break down the tenets of creating good goals. SMART stands for specific, measurable, achievable, relevant, and time-bound.

When creating goals, you must first ensure that you are specific about what you want to achieve. This is one of the most common mistakes people make when creating goals. I hear things like, "I want to do better in school," "I want to make more money," or "I want to be healthier." And these are good desires that are achievable, but they're not specific at all. It's very difficult to know what doing better in school means to everyone. Does it mean getting more A's than B's, no more missing classes, avoiding getting suspended, or increasing your GPA to a 3.0?

It is difficult for you to accurately assess your progress

in reaching a goal when it's not specific. It can also be a struggle to stay on track as you can change what you mean based on how difficult it has been for you to accomplish your goal. This usually cheats you out of your potential by allowing you to continually lower the bar every time there is a barrier in your way. This is an easy trap that sets you up to not hold yourself accountable for reaching your goals.

When deciding if your goal is specific or not, you must ask yourself, "If 20 people heard about my goal, would they all be able to easily tell whether I have successfully completed it or not?" Examples of specific goals may sound like, "I want to stop smoking by January 1st," "I want to get a 3.0 or higher GPA this semester," or "I want to save 5,000 bucks by July 1st." Being specific is the first step to creating well-written goals.

The second step to developing a well-written goal is to make sure it is measurable. Another common mistake that people make is not considering the indicators that will show them they are on track to achieve their goals. If, for instance, someone had the goal of wanting to be healthier—which is not a specific goal—it would be difficult for them to track their progress over time. For some people, being healthier means drinking more water on a consistent basis; for others, it might mean gaining or losing weight.

Mastering Your Process

To ensure that your goal is measurable, you must first ensure that it is specific; then, you must give yourself some milestones to meet along the way, so you can check in and see if you're getting closer to your goal. When goals are measurable, you're able to make adjustments when things aren't on track. For example, if someone wanted to be healthier and decided their specific goal was to lose 16 pounds over two months, that would be easy to track. Over two months, you would have approximately eight weeks total to reach your goal. That means, ideally, you'd lose two pounds each week, and to see if you are on track, you could weigh yourself weekly. If you weighed in at the four-week mark and noticed you had only lost one pound, you could then make some adjustments to your efforts to try to increase the rate you're losing weight at. Your adjustment may be to add another workout day, decrease the number of calories you intake, or improve your sleep. Regardless of what you decide, being able to track your goal allows you to adjust your efforts so you can reach your goal by your desired date, even if you run into some obstacles.

The next aspect of setting a great goal is a little more difficult to incorporate. Making sure your goal is achievable is extremely important, but you don't want it to be so easily attainable that it doesn't help you grow or reach your full potential. This can be tricky as you want to make sure your goal is something that is within your reach without making it something that is so easy to accomplish that it isn't even worth being a goal.

For example, if you are someone who works out in the weight room four to five times a week on a regular basis and currently bench presses a max of 200 pounds, it would be a very low goal to say you want to increase your max to 205 pounds in 12 months. Yes, this would show some growth, and it is specific and measurable, but when you really look at it…is it a big enough goal to make you feel like you're maximizing your potential?

One of the most important things about setting goals that are important to us is to make sure they are worth it. To do this, you want to ask yourself, "Am I pushing myself?" "Is this worth the amount of work and time it's going to take for me to accomplish the goal?" and "Am I setting the bar low so I can easily attain the goal and make myself feel better?"

Although it may not be difficult to move to the 205-pound max, staying focused on a goal for a year does take a lot of effort. If you are doing your regular check-ins and really focusing on your progress, this would be a waste of your time due to the minimal gains you'd achieve.

When making sure goals are achievable, you still want

to make sure you are pushing yourself. When evaluating what is achievable and what is considered pushing yourself, sometimes you must look at what you have already achieved. Using the previous example, if you had increased your max bench by 50 pounds over the *last* 12 months, you might want to set the same goal for the next 12 months. When lifting weights, this can be difficult as we all have some max potential that will hit a cap. But based on your previous gains from this example, you should push yourself to have *at least* the same gains during a similar timeframe.

The fourth aspect of developing a solid goal is to ensure that it is relevant to the things that are most important to you. When looking at the goal, you must ask yourself, "Why is this something I want to achieve?" and "How does this fit into the big picture of my world and/or life?" If I wanted to save a specific amount of money over a period of time, I'd ask myself if that would improve my overall financial wealth and/or life. These types of questions really get to the motivation of creating the goal.

We all have moments when we are charged up and can turn that energy into action—when we feel like we can accomplish many things. In these moments, we are good at creating great goals. The difficult part is when this motivation or energy goes away; what do you do then?

Christopher Robinson

When you make sure your goals are relevant to a bigger picture, you can always refer to your reasoning for making the goal in the first place. This can help drive you through those difficult moments of low energy. For instance, if I needed to save a specific amount of money over a period of time to increase my options in regard to purchasing a house—which in the bigger picture would improve the area my family and I live in—I could always draw on that motivation.

One of the most common questions I ask my clients when they start to deviate from a goal in therapy is, "Why is this goal still important to you?" If they can't answer this question with things that are meaningful and valuable to them in the big scheme of things, they will likely deviate from their plans and discontinue their efforts toward reaching their goal. This is something important that gets skipped when people are excited about setting goals. Really understanding how your goals fit in the big picture of your world is extremely important and will increase the likelihood of you achieving them regardless of what obstacles may come about.

The easiest way to set yourself up not to achieve your goal is to procrastinate. Most of us have experienced this at one time or another. I have repeatedly told myself, "I will get out to mow the lawn at some point" and "I will go back to school to get my master's eventually." To really hold yourself accountable, though, it is essential to establish a realistic timeframe in which the goal should be met. The aspect of goals being time-bound puts unconscious pressure on you to focus on your goal, so it doesn't fall by the wayside. This, simply put, is the easiest step at the end of every goal that you set.

You want to make sure that you have a designated amount of time to accomplish all the steps needed to make sure your desired outcome is reached. Similar to the achievable aspect, you want to make sure that you aren't making it too easy. Instead, you want to consistently push yourself so you can continue to grow.

For example, if I needed to put aside $1,000 in my savings, and I had the ability to save $200 every two weeks, it would be lazy for me to say I want to save $1,000 in 12 months. I have the capacity to save $1,000 after ten weeks, but instead of pushing myself, I am giving myself 52 weeks to save the $1,000. If you understand your habits and know yourself, it is okay to give yourself a cushion and maybe say, "I want to save $1,000 over 12-14 weeks." But to give yourself such a large cushion of 52 weeks will increase the likelihood of procrastination because it unconsciously tells your mind, "I have all year to accomplish my goal."

Now that we have a good understanding of what a productive goal looks like, we can outline some of the main benefits. One of the great benefits of being outcome-driven and creating SMART goals is having an increased focus on the destination you are headed to. Many of us have heard the quote by Yogi Berra that goes, "If you don't know where you're going, you'll end up someplace else." Simply put, if you don't know what you're trying to achieve, you may end up with an outcome you don't want.

Think about it. If you don't outline early in your adult life what you want to do for a career and instead just work meaningless jobs, you may look up with a lot of regret 20-30 years down the line. If you never give yourself any direction regarding what you want to do for a living, there is a good chance that you'll just work jobs that you don't enjoy. We spend so much time working that it's important to do something that aligns with our passions, but if you never give this any consideration, you may end up in a job that you resent. And if you are in a job that you resent, this would be the "someplace else" part of Yogi Berra's quote. Being outcome-driven can help you steer clear of these types of life mistakes.

Another great benefit of being outcome-driven and

developing SMART goals is your ability to concisely break down the steps needed to achieve big accomplishments. Imagine, for instance, that you wanted to get your Master's in Business. This would be a big task for anyone, especially someone just starting out in school. It would take several steps to even get started, which could include getting accepted into a master's program, figuring out a way to pay for school, and creating a schedule that can work with your lifestyle. If you can break down all these steps into achievable tasks, then the overall goal of earning your master's becomes realistic and accomplishable rather than remaining just a dream. This can be applied to any outcome that you may want to achieve, from losing weight to becoming a famous singer or attaining a specific job.

One of the most important aspects of achieving a big goal is having the confidence to do so. Breaking down any goal into achievable steps automatically increases the confidence of most individuals. With that confidence, you will take certain steps, and this can create momentum to achieve more and more until the goal is reached. This is another benefit of being outcome-driven.

The last benefit I will highlight is easily being able to identify progress and success. Because SMART goals are so specific, it is very easy to see if you are heading toward your goal and if that goal has been accomplished or not.

Staying with the last example I used, after working toward that goal for a period of months, you would know if you were on track to earn your master's. You could simply assess your progress by asking yourself, "Am I enrolled in school?" and/or "Am I earning the grades necessary to receive credits toward graduation?"

Let's say you gave yourself a timeframe of three years to earn your master's. If you have not gotten your master's after being in the program for the designated three years, you'll know that you haven't reached your goal. On the contrary, if you *have* graduated and obtained your degree within this timeframe, then this goal has been successfully met. There would be no confusion surrounding whether you have had success or not. Being clear about what you have achieved can continue to help you grow personally with your confidence and self-esteem. These characteristics can aid us as we continue to grow as individuals.

The benefits that we have outlined are not an all-inclusive list. These are just a few of the important benefits of being outcome-driven and developing and working toward SMART goals.

CHAPTER 2 KEY POINTS:

- To create solid outcome-driven goals, be sure to consider the SMART acronym:

    o Specific

    o Measurable

    o Achievable

    o Relevant

    o Time-Bound

- Outcome-driven goals have multiple benefits. Some include:

    o Increased focus and clarity on what you are attempting to accomplish.

    o A way to concisely outline steps to achieve your overall goal.

    o A clear way to recognize progress and success surrounding your desired outcome.

Outcome-Driven Goal Diagram

CHAPTER 3: UNINTENDED CONSEQUENCES OF BEING OUTCOME-DRIVEN

As beneficial as it is to be outcome-driven, there are a lot of pitfalls with this mindset that we usually don't consider, and this can hinder our progress in many areas. Being outcome-driven gives you a clear outline of where you are going—something most people consider a good thing. But one of the issues with being hyper-focused on your destination is that it encourages blinders on your journey.

Imagine this: you're hungry, and there's a place ten miles up the road that sells burgers. Burgers aren't your favorite meal, but you feel like one will do for the time being as it is affordable, and it's not like you *hate* burgers. You only have a bike, and you have made up your mind that you're going to ride it those ten miles to get something to eat. You are very determined, and you've set a time at which you plan to be there to get the burgers. You have outlined all the steps, including getting your money, finding your AirPods so you can listen to music on the way, and ensuring that your bike tires have air in them.

You are extremely focused when you take off to go get your dinner. You have done a good job of zoning out and only focusing on the journey to the restaurant, which helps the time pass. You make it to the place, order your food, and have dinner. You *absolutely* achieved your goal, but here is what you missed:

Being so focused on getting to your destination, you didn't pay attention to the 20 other food places along the way. Being zoned out and only focused on the end goal can create a situation where you miss out on better opportunities. The other 20 potential stops likely had better food choices, more affordable prices, and a much shorter ride—which would have given you more time to do other things that evening.

See, being driven to a specific outcome can make us put on blinders to other potential opportunities. This is one of the unintended consequences of being strictly outcome-driven.

Another thing to consider when emphasizing outcome-driven goals is the issue of being limited to two possible outcomes: failure or success. There are two main issues with this, one being you never want to set yourself up for failure. This can encourage you to set goals that you know are achievable and discourage you from reaching for goals that appear to be too hard, which can leave a lot of your potential on the table since you're not pushing yourself. The other issue with this frame of thinking is that even if you make a lot of progress toward a goal, if you don't achieve it, all of that progress can still feel like a failure. And when you feel like you've failed, you can lose a lot of motivation when it comes to setting future goals.

Imagine you're a high school senior who set a goal to be accepted into Harvard Law School. This is a high-level goal, as Harvard is one of the most difficult schools to be accepted into. Imagine you work extremely hard to keep your grades up, do well on the ACT, and spend *hours* volunteering to improve your chances of acceptance. After a year of hard work and maintaining a 3.9 GPA, you learn that you are not accepted into Harvard.

Overall, you have made a lot of progress as a young person trying to achieve a very high-level goal, but that is not what you're thinking about. All you're worried about is the fact that you didn't make it to the finish line. All that hard work, and you didn't achieve your goal. These types of moments lead people to say things like, "I did all of that for nothing" and "What a waste of time." This defeating feeling eats at our motivation and can lead to us putting in less effort in the future when it comes to other things that are important to us.

Another common pitfall to being outcome-driven is the "What now?" phenomenon. This is usually what we say to ourselves after the great feeling of completing a huge goal is gone. Once you have achieved what you set out to achieve, you get to a crossroads in which you must make new goals or risk losing the benefits of achieving your original goal.

For example, imagine someone setting a goal to lose 50 pounds in six months so they can fit in their new dress for their high school reunion. They make a very good plan—they get a gym membership, input their workout schedule into their calendar, join a nutrition group, and share their goal with their significant other for support. The weekend before their class reunion, they get on the scale, try on their dress, and realize they've hit all their objectives. The goal is completed, and they have an amazing time showing off their new look at their class reunion.

Mastering Your Process

Once the weekend is over, they wake up on Monday and ask themselves, "What now?" They are now at a point where they have to decide what they want to do next and why. Do they want to continue to lose weight? Are they now going to maintain their current weight? Do they set another deadline for when they want to look a certain way for a different event? This can be a difficult moment because if they don't find some highly motivating factors, such as their class reunion, they may not have much of a reason to continue their rigorous weight loss regimen that they stuck to over the last six months.

This is a very common issue. I'm sure you've seen many people lose a significant amount of weight for whatever motivating reason and then gain it all back after they hit their goal within their timeframe. If you can't find a new motivating factor for a goal that you've achieved, then there's a big chance you'll lose the progress you made working toward whatever goal you reached.

This is something that happens a lot, not only for people who set goals to lose weight but also for those who want to save money. They do everything they have to do to save that money for their new house, but once they buy the house and that goal timeline passes, they go back to their old habits if they don't establish a new goal.

The last unintended consequence of being outcome-driven that we will highlight is the negative effect of the deadlines that you give yourself. The benefit of having a deadline is that it protects you from procrastination, but the flip side of that is the risk of encouraging desperation. There can be a fine line between whether a deadline is a benefit or a disadvantage.

Take someone who is searching for a job, for example. Let's say that they gave themselves two months to find an employer, and they are now 45 days into their goal. They have submitted multiple applications, called each job to follow up on those applications, and maintained a consistent job search throughout the process. They have yet to get a job interview, and now they're beginning to feel the pressures of potentially failing their goal at the two-month mark. Although it appears that they have done everything within their power up until this point, the fear of failing has created an anxiety that they don't want to face. This has led to desperation, and now they have decided to lie on

Mastering Your Process

their next few applications to appear more qualified for positions they have not been getting calls back for.

Some will say this is a means to an end, and I can understand that thought process as well. So, this is not to say that lying on applications is right or wrong. It is to say that due to the pressures of wanting to achieve their goal, this hypothetical person has now put themselves into a situation where they may not have considered the potential outcomes of lying. Have they thought about what they would do if they were offered the job and the company found out that they were lying? Have they considered that they now must maintain that lie, and they have to remember it if they're hired?

They may have thought about the pros and cons of their decision, but there's always an increased risk of poor outcomes when people decide to use a desperate tactic to try to meet their goal by its deadline. When we are desperate, we don't consider the potential outcomes of our decisions. We just focus on what we are trying to achieve and do whatever we think we need to do to make it happen. This can lead to significant consequences that we are not prepared for.

In Chapter 1, we discussed 50 Cent and his desire

to "get rich or die trying." As previously highlighted, he created a song titled "Ghetto Quran." As the story goes, this song was made to create interest within the community and increase the potential sales of his album. This song was rumored to be offensive to some very dangerous people in his neighborhood and contributed to him being shot nine times. He survived the attack and has since gone on to speak about this story on many occasions.

In this example, though, 50 Cent appeared to be outcome-driven and desperate to attain success, so much so that he may not have considered the possible risk of being murdered over the content of his song. Some will say this is worth the risk, but that is, of course, after the fact. In such a dangerous situation, you may not want to risk your life if you can find another way to reach your goal.

Let's think back to the Bernie Madoff example from Chapter 1 too. He appeared to be outcome-driven to become extremely wealthy and influential in his industry. However, once his Ponzi scheme was exposed, all that he worked for came crashing down. He was eventually convicted of 11 federal crimes, sentenced to 150 years in prison, and ordered to pay $170 billion in restitution to his victims. He spent a little over 12 years in prison before dying in 2021.

Bernie's family was also impacted in a negative way due to how he decided to attain his wealth. The public was very upset with him and his entire family due to his fraudulent scheme. His brother, Peter, received a ten-year prison sentence for his involvement. And his son, Mark, died of suicide in 2010 after allegedly struggling to adjust to all the negativity attached to his father's legacy.

When considering the cost of everything Bernie gave up and the impact on his family, it is my assumption that if he could do it all over again, he would evaluate the pros and cons of how he attained his wealth and consider if it was worth the effect it had on him and his family.

CHAPTER 3 KEY POINTS:

- Some of the disadvantages of having an outcome-driven mindset include:

    o Having "blinders" on as you focus on the outcome. This can possibly cause you to miss opportunities along the way.

    o Limiting your perspective to either having a successful outcome or failing. There is no in-between.

    o After completing an outcome-driven goal, you must find new motivation and/or a new goal, or you risk losing the benefits of your achievement.

    o When overemphasizing the need to complete the goal, you can fail to assess accurately the risk of *how* you achieve the goal. This can lead to unintended consequences.

CHAPTER 4: BECOMING PROCESS-DRIVEN

When shifting your mindset to becoming more process-driven rather than outcome-driven, you must focus more on the "how" and less on the desired outcome. This pertains to the habits that we have when it comes to certain desires. A habit is something that is a consistent and regular practice, and it's usually difficult to give up because it's typically done unconsciously at times. Focusing on the process means focusing on the journey and not just the destination.

Consider someone running a marathon. They are focusing on *how* they run—ensuring they are consistent with a pace that works for them. They may also be focused on their breathing so they don't push themselves too hard and have to quit from exhaustion. Now, imagine if they just focused on the destination: the finish line. It could be overwhelming to look that far ahead.

But if they focus on the process and the *how*—pacing themselves and breathing properly—finishing the race will happen. Finishing the race was not their goal; their goal was to run at a consistent pace and control their breathing, but they still got the additional result of finishing the race. We consider this a pro of established habits.

Let's look at another example of someone wanting to save money. If someone said they wanted to save money for a house, that would be considered their desired outcome. If they were process-driven, they would ask themself, "What habits do I need to practice to be able to save enough money for a home?" Their goal would then be to establish those habits. That could look like putting 25% of their checks in their savings, eating out no more than once a week, riding their bike to work when the weather permits, or reviewing their household budget monthly. There wouldn't necessarily be a timeline to establish those habits, nor would there be an end destination of saving a certain amount of money. But by establishing these habits and being consistent, they will achieve their process goals.

One major difference between a process and an outcome goal is that an outcome goal can be achieved. A process goal, on the other hand, is something that

Mastering Your Process

you are either doing or not doing. Due to it not being something that can be "finished," it is a constant action. That does not mean every process goal is permanent. Just like habits, process goals can change and adjust.

By the person in our example achieving their goal of establishing these habits, they will get additional positive results, such as the ability to buy a house. Due to the goals not being "finished," they'll continue to benefit from these habits they've established even after they purchase a home. So, not only will they be able to buy a house, but they will also have the ability to manage the new bills that come with owning a home over time. Or if they choose to wait and continue to save, they may even be able to afford a more expensive home.

Another important aspect of being process-driven is how you assess the success of your goals. It is much easier to measure the success of an outcome-driven goal because you can clearly see if you have achieved it within the timeline you established. When assessing the success of establishing new habits, there are a few things to look at. The first thing is whether the habits you wish to establish have become consistent.

Many have heard of the 21-day rule regarding creating habits. It basically states that to establish a habit, you need to do the same thing for 21 days. However, research shows that it takes, on average, a little more than two months to establish a habit. Now, this is not an exact science, and there are many things to take into consideration when trying to establish habits, such as resources, determination, and motivation. Although you don't have a deadline to establish a habit when you're process-driven, it is a good idea to have checkpoints throughout the process to ensure you're consistently practicing the right actions for your desired results.

For example, if I wanted to save 25% of my check on a consistent basis, I could review my bank statements from the last 30-60 days to ensure I've been doing this. My level of success is for me to decide, but the more that I see I am doing this, the more successful I am. If there was one pay period in which I did not save 25%, it doesn't automatically mean that I have failed. This is different from an outcome goal, where you have a desired result you're working toward and most people consider it a failure if they don't reach it.

When looking at process-driven goals, you may

just feel more successful if you have done the action steps more times than not. This increases motivation as you move forward. If you aren't completing the steps often, you can always adjust whatever is necessary to help you. In my example, I may want to save a lesser percentage of my salary or increase my income by getting a part-time job if I struggle to consistently save 25% of my checks.

The next aspects to focus on when evaluating your success in achieving your process goals are the pros and cons of your habits. Due to process goals not having an established end date, it is important to do this to ensure that you are getting what you want out of the habits you have established. Establishing new habits to achieve the outcomes that you want can be extremely beneficial, but doing this without evaluating the pros and cons can have unintended consequences.

For example, let's say you created a great work-life balance by working 60 hours a week, making time to connect with your friends by playing video games on the weekend, and exercising for two hours a day, six days a week (taking Sundays off). When looking at the pros and cons of these habits, you determined that the pros far outweighed the cons and decided to keep these practices intact. Fast forward three years of having these habits in place, and now you are getting ready to be married and have a child. Some might say, "I'm not giving up what works for me for someone else." But when weighing the pros and cons of what is most important to you, some adjustments may be necessary.

That doesn't mean you can't prioritize what's important regarding your self-care; it just means you may have to establish new habits for your relationship and your new journey into parenthood. This would mean that some of your process goals would need to be adjusted or completely discontinued.

One thing about life is if you are here long enough, you are guaranteed to see some things change. Very few things stay the exact same forever. Due to process goals generally being long-term, it is important to consistently assess the pros and cons of your habits to make sure you're getting the most benefits possible and managing any disadvantages that might cause issues.

If the cons ever outweigh the pros, you should either make adjustments or stop that habit completely. If the pros continue to outweigh the cons, then you should continue practicing the habit and decide if it is well-established. If it is well-established, you can then add more habits to increase the chances of your overall desired outcome and repeat the cycle with new habits. Refer to the "Process Goal Diagram" at the end of the chapter to see how all the steps come together.

It takes a mental shift for most of us to focus on the process rather than reach for our dreams. When focusing on the process, you do not disregard your dreams; you pay more attention to how you are doing things that lead to your dreams. It's a constant flow; there's no desginated end like there is with outcome-driven goals.

It's important to highlight that there are process goals that are short-term and can be done for a designated amount of time. For clarity, in this book, we are focusing on long-term actions that become habits. So, while you are reading this book, think of the big-picture things you want to achieve in your relationships, careers, or other areas of your life.

CHAPTER 4 KEY POINTS:

- Being process-driven emphasizes how you do things rather than focusing on the outcome.

- On average, it takes a little more than two months to establish a habit.

- When creating process-driven goals (habits), you must assess if you are consistently taking the steps you outline, and you must regularly examine the pros and cons of the habits, as they can change.

Mastering Your Process

Process Goal Diagram

CHAPTER 5: BENEFITS OF BEING PROCESS-DRIVEN

Now that we have a solid understanding of what being process-driven means and how this mindset can be used to establish habits, let's highlight some of the benefits of having this mindset.

Unlike being outcome-driven, when you're process-driven, there is no specific designated end to a habit you establish. You focus more on the action of doing something instead of trying to get somewhere. Due to there not being any specific end, you are less likely to develop anxiety or frustration about not reaching your end goal.

Now, when establishing these habits, or process goals, there's the expectation that there will be benefits. These benefits can be the outcomes that you initially wanted to achieve when you were more outcome-driven. For example, if you wanted to save a certain amount of money to purchase a home, this would be considered your desired outcome. If shifting

Mastering Your Process

to be more process-driven, you would establish habits that increase the likelihood of you having money for a home. Purchasing a house would not be your end goal, though; it would just be one of the potential results of the habits that you put in place.

When establishing these types of habits, in most cases, you have no reason to stop or refocus them once you get your desired outcome(s). However, when you are outcome-driven and you get the result you want, you usually must refocus and figure out your next goal. So, if you worked extremely hard to save up enough money for a house, once you purchase that home, you'll probably have to figure out another motivating factor or reason to continue to save.

But when you have established a habit of saving—without any specific reason—you can purchase a home *and* investigate more opportunities you might be able to afford due to you consistently saving money. See, with a process-driven mindset, your goal is to establish the habit of saving, not to necessarily purchase a house, but if you are meeting that goal of saving, you will always have the option to purchase things such as a home.

Another benefit to being more process-driven is

that this way of thinking allows you the open-mindedness needed to see all the potential advantages of the habits that you establish. When outcome-driven, you're so focused on one specific outcome that you may not necessarily notice other possibilities or take advantage of other options along the way. However, when your focus is more on the habit that you have established and you take the opportunity to assess the pros of that habit, you are able to clearly see the benefits of practicing that behavior. That means the habits you establish can provide you with more benefits than just the one outcome you may want. As you consistently establish new habits to help you achieve the things that are important to you, you can assess the outcomes that you get, even if they're not the specific ones you're focused on.

For example, if you establish a healthy habit of consistently saving money, the goal is simply to save, not to save for a specific item. However, after doing this for several years, you'll be able to buy a car off the lot with no monthly payment, put a down payment on a new home and have a more affordable mortgage, or pay for your children's college expenses. And although these are amazing outcomes, none of them were your goal. These are just examples of the positive results

Mastering Your Process

that can happen when you establish a healthy habit. The habit was the goal, and these potential outcomes are opportunities that you can take advantage of due to practicing that habit.

The other side to being able to assess the pros of a habit is the ability to assess the cons as well. People who are very successful and outcome-driven often have the frame of mind that they will achieve their goals by any means necessary. This can lead to serious unintended consequences as they are hyper-focused on their desired outcome. However, when assessing the pros of a habit, we also assess the cons, and this is not something that happens only once because habits can be established and practiced for years or a lifetime. To ensure habits are beneficial for you, it is important to assess not only the pros of those habits but also the cons. If at any point the cons or risks of practicing a habit become greater than the pros, it is encouraged to consider adjusting your habit or completely discontinuing it.

Let's say, for example, that you have established a great routine for yourself that consists of early morning workouts, weekly mental health therapy, 60-hour work weeks, and at least six solo vacations a year.

Imagine you have this routine, and it has been great for your overall self-care. You have made a point to assess the pros and cons of these habits on a regular basis, and you always see that the pros rank much higher than the cons.

Let's say that you had this routine when you were a single individual. Over the next year, you establish a serious intimate relationship, and now you have a newborn on the way. As you assess these habits, you see that the cons rank much higher than they did in the past. You no longer have as much free time because now you need to invest time into a family that means a lot to you.

This could require you to adjust your habits by decreasing your solo vacations, adding some family vacations, and/or attending couples therapy in addition to individual therapy. Regardless, due to you consistently assessing your habits, you can identify the potential risks of continuing to practice them without accounting for your new committed relationship or child on the way.

Imagine if Bernie Madoff considered the pros and cons of the habits that he established to make him so wealthy. If he had honestly considered the worst that could have happened, there's a great chance that he would've chosen different habits. Although he attained great wealth, how he did it cost him his freedom and played a role in the suicide of one of his children. It's hard to tell what he was thinking, but it can be assumed by looking at his overall goal of having such great wealth that he was very outcome-driven.

Assessing your cons gives you the opportunity to adjust where needed. When looking at the "Process Goal Diagram" from the previous chapter, you see there is a step in which you must decide to either continue, adjust, or completely stop your habit(s). It is encouraged to assess the pros and cons on a regular basis, such as every three to six months or less. This allows you to foresee what the long-term implications may be if you don't make changes to what you've done in the past.

To understand the last benefit that we will highlight, consider the difference between someone who wants to get in shape and someone who lives a healthy lifestyle. On the surface, both individuals may do a lot of the same things, such as lift weights, count their calories, jog, and ensure they get seven to eight hours of sleep a night. So, if you're watching both individuals focus on their goals, it can be difficult to decipher the differences.

The main difference between these individuals is that the person who's trying to get in shape is working toward a desired outcome. This, once again, fosters attention and clarity surrounding when they have or haven't achieved their goal. The person who wants to live a healthy lifestyle, on the other hand, does all the same things but is less likely to lose motivation, as a healthy lifestyle is something that is ongoing and doesn't have an end result.

When focused on establishing habits that lead to positive outcomes, the action steps can become easier and feel like they require less effort. When you do not attach those habits to an end result, that motivation to continue to do them can unconsciously remain. On the contrary, when there is an outcome that you are looking forward to, there is a good chance that your motivation will have to be reactivated after you achieve the goal.

Think of something that requires a lot of your focus—something that requires you to be consciously present when doing it. This is usually some type of tedious task. It takes a lot more brainpower and sometimes physical effort to complete this type of task. When you are done, you may feel drained, even if it was something that didn't take a lot of physical strength. An example of this type of task may be multiple hours of data entry or writing a college research paper. Usually, when you have these kinds of tasks, you look forward to finishing them and dread the next time you'll have to do them.

Now think about tasks that you can practically do in your sleep—tasks that don't necessarily require you to pay attention to what you're doing because you can get through them unconsciously. These tasks usually take little energy because they can basically be done on autopilot. For some, this could be cleaning your house. If you're an athlete, it might be you playing in an actual game. And for others, it could be driving a long distance for a vacation. The point is this task doesn't appear daunting to you, nor does it put you in a situation where you feel like you just want to be done with it.

Given that outcome-driven goals take a lot of focus, it can make you feel like the task is tedious and draining. However, once habits are established, they can be done without a lot of focus. This means they require less energy. Now, that's not to say that you don't focus on your habits or that they don't drain you at times. It's to say that it will almost always require *more* mental focus and emotional energy to reach one specific desired outcome than it will to consistently practice a well-established habit.

CHAPTER 5 KEY POINTS:

- Being process-driven helps you avoid the anxiety of a deadline.

- Establishing habits instead of seeking outcomes can result in additional benefits that you didn't initially expect.

- Assessing the cons of a new habit can help avoid unintended consequences.

- Well-established habits can require less energy and motivation than an outcome-driven goal.

CHAPTER 6: USING OUTCOMES TO ESTABLISH YOUR PROCESS

At this point, you may be asking yourself, "Should I just throw away all my dreams and forget about everything I want to achieve?" And the answer is, "of course not." That wouldn't make much sense, nor would it motivate many people to engage in a more process-driven way of thinking. What you should do instead is allow your dreams and outcome-driven goals to drive your process. This may require some time and exploration, but eventually, it can lead to established habits that will benefit you for a lifetime.

Start with listing your dreams. The good thing about dreams is that they don't have to be as specific as an outcome-driven goal. You can just list very general objectives. You can say things such as "I want to be healthier and stronger," "I want to be better with my money," "I want to have a better marriage," or "I want to be better when it comes to managing my mental health."

Mastering Your Process

When outlining what your dreams are, you want to explore the habits of people who have achieved similar things. This can be a very easy process if you have someone you look up to who can share some of their habits and the pros and cons of them with you. This person could be a mentor, parent, sibling, coworker, or supervisor. Just remember, what you aspire to achieve should dictate whom you look to.

A lot of people reading this book already know what habits they need to implement to get the outcomes they want; they just haven't been able to consistently establish them for whatever reason. If that is you, try shifting the way you look at your goals; focus more on the habits and less on the actual outcome. Sometimes it's difficult to achieve an outcome-driven goal because of how overwhelming it seems. Focusing on just the habits linked to that potential outcome instead can boost your confidence.

Just like any type of goal, if you can create momentum, it is easier to tackle the steps that lie ahead. With process goals, you can assess if you're consistently taking the steps that you outlined for yourself, and if you are, that is considered a success. You may not have started to see the benefits of the habit you are establishing, such as saving a large sum of money, but you aren't focused primarily on the outcome(s)—you're focused on practicing the habit, so you gain momentum by celebrating your consistency.

Process goals don't set you up to quickly get what you want. Instead, they establish a foundation for you to achieve many things, even those you may not have considered

***

Now, the one thing you want to avoid with a process-driven mindset is focusing on too many habits at once. If, for instance, you explore habits that can improve your relationship with your partner and you see that there are six to seven practices you want to adopt, it can be overwhelming to try to implement them all at the same time. Now, this doesn't mean you can't intentionally make multiple efforts at once. It's just that if you focus on adopting six to seven habits/process goals at the same time, you'll likely feel overwhelmed—decreasing your likelihood of success. A good starting place is to look at one or two—but no

Mastering Your Process

more than three—habits to focus on at a time.

To improve your relationship, these habits may include having regular check-ins with your partner to discuss your two's feelings, agreeing on how to resolve conflict, and an arranged amount of time for each of you to spend with friends away from each other. Doing these three things wouldn't guarantee a perfect relationship, but if done on a consistent basis, they could lead to some positive outcomes, such as having better conflict resolution skills and being more connected as a couple. After attempting to establish these habits for an agreed-upon amount of time, you would then assess how consistent you both have been as a couple in implementing them. And once you've done that, it's time to assess the pros and cons of the habits.

It's important to first ascertain your consistency in practicing the habits because if you try to evaluate their benefits without fully implementing them, you might misinterpret the results. In essence, it would be like working part-time but expecting to be paid as a full-time employee. You shouldn't expect full-time pay until you work full-time hours. This is the same way you must view the potential pros of your habits—you can't expect any benefits without consistency. So, before you can correctly assess the pros and cons, you have to ensure the habits are practiced on a regular basis.

If you determine the habits to be inconsistent, you must take time to address this before assessing the pros and cons. At this stage, you may decide to focus on decreasing the number of habits you want to establish, adding some reminders to help you be more consistent, or using a new strategy, such as couples counseling, to further assist you. It is common at this stage for people to give up due to obstacles. That's why it's important for you to revisit your motivating factors for establishing these habits in the first place.

Using the same example from above, why were you motivated to save your relationship? Did your motivation come from a desire to be happier at home? Or was it a more selfless reason, like helping your partner feel more joy? In this phase, it is always important to answer your why, as this can help re-motivate you to focus on problem-solving and prevent you from discontinuing a habit that could potentially help you.

Once you determine that the habits are practiced consistently, you can move on to assess their pros and cons. If the habits show more pros than cons, contin-

Mastering Your Process

ue to do them. If you see that the habits have more cons than pros, either adjust the habit or discontinue it. This is a very important stage, as there are times when habits only *look* like they're going to help you. So by consistently assessing the pros and cons, you can forego the potential risks and/or consequences that you didn't consider when first adopting your habits. Just because you decide that a habit is no longer beneficial to you does not mean you stop wanting the desired outcome of an improved relationship. At this stage, you just need to consider other habits without risks that might render better results.

Remember, it takes about two months on average to establish a habit. That makes two months a good checkpoint to see if a new desired behavior has become a habit. You can use the following questions to evaluate if a behavior has truly become a habit:

Do I complete the desired behavior on a consistent basis?

Do I complete the behavior unconsciously?

Does practicing the behavior require less effort than it did when I first established it?

If the answer is "no" to any of these questions, continue to focus on establishing the habit until the answer is "yes." At this point, you should resolve any problems getting in the way of you establishing the habit. If there are no issues to resolve, continue with the process. Once you can honestly answer "yes" to all the questions, you can focus on two to three more habits that will increase the likelihood of your original desired outcome: improving your relationship with your partner. You would follow the exact same process to establish and evaluate future habits.

Utilizing this process for important goals can help people achieve the outcomes that they desire *and* adopt positive habits that lead to even more than they imagined. Focusing on the habits that will generate the results you want increases the likelihood of long-term success and saves you from having to figure out what race to run next when you cross the finish line.

CHAPTER 6 KEY POINTS:

- It's important to explore what habits are needed to achieve the dreams and outcomes we desire.

- Celebrating the consistency of practicing a new habit will create momentum for establishing more habits that contribute to your desired outcomes and dreams.

- Avoid trying to establish more than three habits at a time, as this can be overwhelming and decrease the likelihood of success.

CHAPTER 7: PEOPLE SUCCESSFULLY MASTERING THEIR PROCESS

In this chapter, we will explore two individuals and one couple who have used a process-driven mindset to achieve the outcomes that they desired. Their process will be outlined using the process goal cycle described in Chapter 4.

KEISHA, AGE 33, SINGLE MOTHER WITH THREE KIDS, FACTORY WORKER

<u>Initial Desired Outcomes/Dreams</u>

Keisha is a hard-working mother who has expressed desires for more financial flexibility, an increase in her savings, her first house, and a newer car. She explained that she has some issues with her credit and very little in her savings, but she has recently start-

Mastering Your Process

ed a new job as a factory worker. She has been making enough to cover all her bills and has plenty left over for savings, but she cannot seem to save consistently.

When exploring her account history, she notices that she spends quite a bit on eating out during the week and on recreational activities such as movies with her kids or going out with her friends on the weekends. She also sees that she uses her credit cards too often and that she always has to dedicate a large portion of her paychecks to catch up.

Keisha expressed that trying to increase her credit score by 100 points has been overwhelming, as it seems to go up very slowly and down very quickly. This has decreased her motivation in the past, even though she knows she needs a higher score to purchase a new home and car. She also has been very unmotivated to save 10k for a down payment on a house, as that seems like more money than she would ever be able to save.

Before moving forward and deciding the necessary steps to increase the likelihood that she achieves her dreams, Keisha was first encouraged to highlight her reasons for desiring these outcomes. She emphasized the importance of being a good example for her children. She expressed how important it was to show her children more possibilities than what she was exposed to.

She mentioned a serious history of depression, which is usually linked to stress. And a huge source of Keisha's stress has always been things associated with finances. She has a history of struggling to pay bills on time and was even evicted once. If she had financial flexibility and security, she feels that her mental health would improve, which would contribute to her being a healthier person overall and a better mother.

Keisha was tasked with creating a list of potential habits that would increase the likelihood of her achieving these outcomes. She took time to read and talk to people who successfully managed their finances to explore the habits she should put in place. She came up with the following list:

- Schedule 10% of every paycheck to automatically deposit into a separate savings account—an account not to be used for regular monthly expenses
- Create a monthly budget to adhere to that includes funds for extracurricular activities such as outings and family events

Mastering Your Process

- Ensure credit card usage is no more than 20% every month

- Meal prep on Sundays to avoid eating out

- Explore higher-paying job opportunities within and outside of current factory company

Now that Keisha has a solid list of habits that can help her achieve her outcomes, it is time for her to select two to three to focus on so she isn't overwhelmed or tempted to rush the process. When deciding what habits she should focus on, Keisha is encouraged to start with those that'll be easiest for her to master. This increases the likelihood that she'll stay on track and helps her create momentum to focus on the other habits that she'll need to master in the future. This is all a preference, of course, but if she were to start with the most difficult habit, it could demotivate her and make it tougher for her to focus on the overall process.

After taking some time to explore, she decided to start by focusing on meal prepping and saving 10% of her paychecks.

Christopher Robinson
Step 1: Put Habits into Practice

To establish the first habit, she makes a list of what she needs to meal prep. She first outlines a schedule for her Sunday. She is always off on Sundays, so she has most of the day for planning. She also has her kids every Sunday, which makes it difficult for her to go to the grocery store. This is the first barrier that she must account for. After some problem-solving, she decides to order groceries instead of physically going to the store.

She downloads the grocery store's app on her phone and sets up an account. She plans to make her grocery list throughout the week by entering food items as she thinks of them. This makes it easier for her to remember what's needed. If she notices a food item, such as milk or sugar, getting low, she can just enter it in her cart on the grocery store's app. She can also explore different meals throughout the week that she sees on TikTok.

If there is anything she wants to try, she can simply enter the ingredients in her cart. By Sunday morning, she'll have most of her grocery list completed, and she can finalize it then. After ordering groceries on Sunday morning, she can expect to have them delivered no later than that afternoon. Keisha plans to meal prep lunch for the work week. She also plans to have easy-to-make breakfast food that she can take in the mornings to avoid stopping at Starbucks or Tim Hortons like she normally does.

The next habit was simpler for Keisha to establish. To save 10% of every paycheck, she first went to a credit union she didn't have an account with and opened a new savings account. She decided that it would be best to use a different credit union instead of her current one so she wouldn't be enticed to transfer money out of the account like she does with her current savings.

She also plans to leave the card for this account at home and not in her purse. This will make the new savings account less accessible, decreasing the likelihood that she spends its money. Lastly, she went to her payroll department and completed the necessary forms to have 10% of her checks automatically deposited into the new account.

Step 2: Assess Consistency of Habits

When establishing her process goals, Keisha set a

checkpoint at every 30 days. This gives her four paychecks to review as well as four weeks to assess how her meal prepping has been going.

At her first 30-day mark, she assessed that she prepped three full weeks of meals that helped her not eat out while at work. During the second week, she wasn't feeling well on Sunday, so she didn't prep any meals. She noticed that she spent more money eating out the first two days of that week and didn't feel good about it. As a result, she made a few cold lunches for the remainder of the week, which she felt were more congruent with her process goals. Overall, it appears that she adhered to her process goals more than not, so in assessing if this goal was on a successful track, she deemed that it was.

Regarding her saving 10% of every paycheck—this has gone well without any deviation. The money has consistently been coming out of her checks, and she hasn't even been paying attention to the savings account. She hasn't used the card attached to the account once, nor has she felt compelled to. So, this goal is also on track. Overall, she is showing consistency in establishing these new habits.

Mastering Your Process
Step 3: Assess Pros and Cons of Habits

Now it's time to assess the pros and cons of both habits Keisha established. Remember, if there was no consistency with the habits when assessed in Step 2, this step could not be completed, as the accuracy of assessing the pros and cons would be affected. When looking at the pros and cons of her two habits, Keisha was able to highlight the following:

Meal Prepping Habit Pros:

- Saving about 60 extra dollars a week on food
- Conserving gas by not leaving work to eat out
- Eating healthier
- Spending time with my oldest meal prepping
- Setting a healthier example for my kids
- Lost 3 pounds this month

Meal Prepping Habit Cons:

- Sundays are busier now
- Miss eating Tim Hortons

- Eating the same meal over and over during the week

Saving 10% from Paycheck Habit Pros:

- Savings account has been consistent for the month
- Closer to dreams of owning a house and a new car
- Takes no effort to put the money away
- Saved $340 so far

Saving 10% from Paycheck Habit Cons:

- Reaching savings goal still feels overwhelming
- Less money for unplanned fun activities

Step 4: Continue or Adjust/Stop Habits

Now that each habit has been assessed for its pros and cons, it's time to decide if the habits are worth continuing, if they need to be adjusted, or if they need to be completely discontinued. Just because a habit has more items listed in the pros doesn't mean the pros rank higher than the cons.

To ascertain if the pros list outweighs the cons list, you must decide which pros are most important to you and which cons are most important to you. Think about it; there may only be one con, but that con can be so important to you that it outweighs the six pros that you're getting. An easy example of this would be if there was something negatively impacting your health listed as a con. For most people, their physical health is much more important than money, fun, or entertainment. So, if this was the case for one of your habits, you may decide to discontinue or adjust it.

Keisha has looked at the pros and cons of meal prepping, and although it requires more energy on her off day, she feels the pros far outweigh the cons. Not only is she saving money like she originally desired, but she has also noticed other benefits of meal prepping. As you may recall, she highlighted how important her children are to her. And now, she is spending more time with her oldest child because of meal prepping. She is also eating healthier, which sets a better example for her children. Although she has not been trying to lose weight, she has, and this is another advantage from her perspective. Due to the current benefits, she has decided to continue this habit.

Now let's look at the 10% she is saving from every paycheck. She feels that the pros far outweigh the cons of this habit as well. However, there is one specific con that she wants to address: the overwhelming feeling that she's a long way from her desired outcome. This concern has motivated her to adjust the habit. Given that she is now saving more money by meal prepping and that she feels saving 10% of her paychecks has been effortless, she has decided to save 15%. That means this habit has been adjusted.

Step 5: Continue/Add Habits and Repeat

At the final stage of this cycle, Keisha must decide if she feels these habits are well-established so she can focus on incorporating more habits from her original list. She has already established that the pros are worth continuing both habits. So, she will now use the following three questions to ascertain if she's ready to add even more habits from her original list.

Mastering Your Process

Meal Prepping Habit:

Do I complete the desired behavior on a consistent basis? **Yes.**

Do I complete the behavior unconsciously? **No, it still takes a lot of focus to complete.**

Does practicing the behavior require less effort than it did when I first established it? **No, it still takes a lot of effort to complete on my days off.**

The meal-prepping habit has made progress and continues to be successful, but according to Keisha, it is not an established habit yet. So, she will focus on this habit, follow the steps in the cycle, and re-assess it in another 30 days.

Saving 10% from Paycheck Habit (Adjusted to 15%):

Do I complete the desired behavior on a consistent basis? **No, this habit has been adjusted and increased from 10% to 15%. At 10%, it was consistent, but 15% is a new standard that has yet to be established.**

Do I complete the behavior unconsciously? **Yes, but it has not been done at 15% yet.**

Does practicing the behavior require less effort than it did when I first established it? **Yes, but it has not been done at 15% yet.**

The saving 10% from every paycheck habit has been successful as well, but it was adjusted. And due to it being adjusted, Keisha does not have an accurate assessment of whether it's an established habit or not. If she hadn't adjusted it, it appears that saving 10% could have passed the standard to be considered a habit, but increasing it means she must wait to see if the 15% is just as consistent and effortless as the 10% was. She will continue to focus on establishing this habit, and she'll follow the steps of this cycle for another 30 days. Due to continuing her focus on both habits, Keisha will not add any new habits at this time; this will help her avoid overwhelming herself.

CAM, AGE 16, JUNIOR IN HIGH SCHOOL, VARSITY BASKETBALL PLAYER

Mastering Your Process
Initial Desired Outcomes/Dreams

Cam is a young man beginning his junior year of high school. He just learned that he made the varsity basketball team, which had been a major goal of his. He has continued to express a desire to play Division I basketball and hopefully earn a chance to play professionally overseas or in the NBA. This has been a dream of his since he was five years old.

Cam has a history of struggling in school due to submitting assignments late, not studying for difficult subjects, and being tardy to class. When he puts in the effort, he consistently gets A's and B's, but when he loses motivation, he gets C's and D's. He seems to be more motivated during basketball season because when his grades drop, he is at risk of being academically ineligible. However, when the season is over, he cares less about his grades. He also enjoys spending time with his friends who aren't on his team, and this distracts him from workouts and studying on the weekends.

Cam expressed the main reason he wants to achieve the dream of playing professional basketball is so he can have a job that he loves and not just feel like he is working for a living. He also explained that he is motivated to go to college and get a degree to set an example for his two younger siblings as the first in his family to attend college.

No one in his family has attended college, and his parents have emphasized how big of a deal it would be if he did. Cam states that a basketball scholarship would increase the likelihood of him being able to afford tuition, so this is added motivation to do well at basketball.

To create a potential list of habits that will increase the likelihood of Cam achieving his dreams, he did some research on three of his favorite NBA players—Damian Lillard, Ja Morant, and Bradley Beal—to learn the behaviors they practiced early in their career and what they do now. He also discussed the behaviors important to his success as a basketball player with his high school coach. He came up with the following list:

- Designate at least three hours a week for homework/studying outside of school

- Review progress reports with all teachers once a week

- Meet with the high school coach weekly to discuss areas for improvement

Mastering Your Process

- Designate at least three hours for personal basketball workouts a week

- Complete strength training at least three days a week

- Monitor daily caloric intake

- Drink a gallon of water a day

- Limit fast food to one time a week

Because he is very motivated, Cam decided to focus on establishing three habits. He started by designating three hours a week for homework/studying, reviewing progress reports with teachers once a week, and completing strength training at least three days a week.

Step 1: Put Habits into Practice

To establish the habit of designating three hours a week for homework/studying, Cam buys a large calendar to put on the wall in his room. He first outlines his obligations, which include school, basketball practice, and games. Once he has all his obligations listed on his calendar, he looks to see what days and times he can consistently commit to studying. He first eliminates early mornings before school because he is not a morning person, and although he feels he won't have a problem getting up, he doesn't think his mind would be clear enough to focus on studying at 5:00 a.m.

He currently has consistent availability on Saturdays and Sundays, so he decides to use these days to his advantage. He schedules time to study and complete homework from 11 a.m.-12 p.m. on these days. And he adds Wednesdays from 8 p.m.-9 p.m. for his final day because it will allow him to focus on homework for the week and study for tests/quizzes he may have on Fridays.

To establish meeting with his teachers weekly, Cam emails them and requests help to review his progress every Friday while in class. Every teacher agrees to his request, and several state they'll provide a full update via email if there's no time to meet during class on Fridays. Cam also adds this weekly progress report check to his large calendar.

To establish his third habit of strength training for three days a week, he meets with his assistant coach to develop a program. The assistant coach creates a personalized routine for Cam to focus on the things that would most benefit his style of play. This program requires about 45 minutes of training for each session. Cam explores his calendar to find what days and times would work for him.

Since his program requires a day of rest after working out, he decides on Monday, Wednesday, and Friday mornings from 5:30 a.m.-6:15 a.m. He plans to work out at the local YMCA because he already has a membership there, and he lives only 10 minutes away. He figures this will give him time to work out, shower, and have breakfast before school.

Cam now has all three of his process goals listed in his large calendar. He also decided to add them to his phone calendar with an alarm as an additional reminder.

Step 2: Assess Consistency of Habits

Cam decided to do a check-in on his habits after 60 days. This gave him eight weeks' worth of effort to assess. By his first check-in, he should have completed a total of 24 hours of studying/homework outside of school. However, he charts that he completed a total of 20 hours. When reviewing reasons for not adhering to his goal, he noticed there were two weekends when he didn't have any homework and didn't take advantage of the time to just study for his classes. Overall, Cam feels he has been consistently adhering to this goal.

During his check-in with his second habit, he saw he successfully reviewed his progress reports with every teacher on Fridays without missing a week. Even when he forgot a few times, his teachers reminded him, and he was able to assess how he was doing in his classes. So, this goal is on track.

However, when it comes to the strength training that he's supposed to do three days a week, he has missed 50% of his workouts. Cam has struggled to consistently get up and have the energy and motivation for strength training. He noticed that over the last two weeks, though, he was able to attend all three days he scheduled for himself. Although Cam has started to show consistency as of late, this goal overall has not been consistent.

Step 3: Assess Pros and Cons of Habits

Three Hours of Homework/Studying Habit Pros:

- Currently has all A's in his classes

- Parents have expressed how proud they are

- Sense of pride in his grades has increased overall

- Less stress about school and no need to cram studying for tests

Three Hours of Homework/Studying Habit Cons:

- Have seen friends less during these past two months

- Some headaches on the weekend when reading too long

Review Progress Report Habit Pros:

- Turning all of his work in on a consistent basis

- Less of an overwhelming feeling balancing all classwork from each class

- Contributing to all A's in his classes

- Staying eligible for basketball games

Review Progress Report Habit Cons:

- Sometimes, it feels like teachers are lecturing about how important schoolwork is

Strength Training Habit Pros:

- N/A: Can't accurately assess the pros and cons due to not consistently adhering to this goal

Strength Training Habit Cons:

- N/A

Step 4: Continue or Adjust/Stop Habits

When assessing the pros and cons of reviewing his progress reports and adhering to his designated studying/homework times, Cam determined that the pros far outweighed the cons. He was able to see that these habits take very little effort and help him maintain great grades. This has increased his confidence regarding what he can achieve in college because he knows he can use the same strategies there to prioritize schoolwork. He will continue to maintain these habits going forward.

Due to not adhering consistently to the strength training program, he could not accurately assess the pros and cons. He did, however, express that he could see a change in his jumping ability and his overall strength when guarding bigger players. Given the small benefits that he observed, he decided that he wanted to continue to work on establishing this habit.

To increase his chances of success, he explores what got in the way of him not going to work out on certain days. As he reflected, he was able to ascertain that his sleep schedule might be contributing to his lack of energy.

He noticed that on days he slept less than six hours, he struggled to go to the YMCA. So, he decided to create a night-time routine to ensure he consistently gets seven to eight hours of sleep. This routine consists of taking melatonin and shutting his phone and TV down at a designated time.

Step 5: Continue/Add Habits and Repeat

At this final stage of the cycle, Cam must decide if he will continue to focus on these three habits or if he is able to add new habits to focus on. He will do this by answering the following three questions for each habit.

Christopher Robinson
3 Hours of Homework/Studying Habit:

Do I complete the desired behavior on a consistent basis? **Yes.**

Do I complete the behavior unconsciously? **Yes.**

Does practicing the behavior require less effort than it did when I first established it? **Yes.**

The three hours of homework/studying a week has been easy for Cam to implement. He feels he is conditioned to go study every time the alarm goes off on his phone. This habit is also consistently in his mind because he sees it on his calendar every day in his room. This is not something he has to continue to focus on as a goal, as it is now an established habit.

Review Progress Report Habit:

Do I complete the desired behavior on a consistent basis? **Yes.**

Do I complete the behavior unconsciously? **Yes.**

Mastering Your Process

Does practicing the behavior require less effort than it did when I first established it? **Yes.**

Like the first habit, this goal has taken little effort to keep in action. Cam feels that he doesn't even have to think about it, as his teachers will remind him if he doesn't bring it up, so this is now an established habit as well.

Strength Training Habit:

Do I complete the desired behavior on a consistent basis? **No.**

Do I complete the behavior unconsciously? **No.**

Does practicing the behavior require less effort than it did when I first established it? **No.**

The strength training habit has begun to show some benefits, but Cam has not consistently maintained it. However, he was able to evaluate the obstacles and come up with a strategy to help him going forward.

He will continue this habit, follow the steps in the cycle, and re-assess in another 60 days.

Cam was able to successfully establish two out of three of his habits. Now he can follow the steps of the cycle and find one to two new habits to incorporate. He will also continue to focus on strength training until it is established as a successful habit.

RICK AND KIM, MARRIED FOR FOUR YEARS, HAVE A ONE-YEAR-OLD CHILD, COLLEGE PROFESSORS.

Initial Desired Outcomes/Dreams

Rick and Kim are a couple entering their fifth year of marriage. As individuals, they are achieving great accomplishments within their respective careers. According to them, their dedication to other priorities as of late has taken their focus away from their marriage. Kim has felt disconnected from Rick since their son was born. Rick has experienced some difficulties connecting with Kim, as she is the main nurturing parent for their child. This causes him to feel neglected at times.

Mastering Your Process

Rick has expressed that he really wants to be a good father and husband and feels he is doing that by conquering his career and providing more financial flexibility for his family. Kim has expressed that she is struggling to balance being a new mother, maintaining her career, and being the partner that she feels Rick wants. They both want to find ways to connect better, improve their overall happiness as a couple, and decrease the tension in their home. They also have a fear of separating if things don't improve.

Rick expressed he is motivated to improve their marriage because of the love he has for his wife and his desire to provide a loving home and family unit for his son. He also believes they can achieve more as a couple than they would as individuals raising a child together.

Kim expressed her reasons for wanting to improve their marriage are her love for her husband, her desire to decrease stress caused by the tension in their home, and her desire to provide a happy family environment for their son.

Over the last few months, things have gotten really frustrating for both Rick and Kim. They appear to argue over the smallest things, including household chores, money, and a lack of affection between the two of them. They recently took a love language assessment and learned that they both have different ways they want to be loved. Kim figured out she really appreciates words of affirmation and acts of service, while Rick values quality time and physical touch. They both feel that they're receiving very little love in the form they desire.

The couple has stated that they really want to figure out a way to reconnect and re-establish the happy marriage that they're used to having. To explore a list of habits that will create a more joyful and harmonious marriage, they started by discussing their situation with the pastor of their church. They also attended a weekend marriage counseling retreat and generated some ideas from that. They came up with the following list:

- Attend weekly marriage counseling
- Schedule and have a date night at least every two weeks
- Attend church together weekly
- Spend 30 minutes a night checking in with each other without phones or distractions

- Rick finds one way per week to provide an "act of service," and Kim finds one way a week to provide "quality time"

- Schedule and have individual self-care time every two weeks, separate from each other

- Create and adhere to a household to-do list (cooking, cleaning, baby needs, laundry, etc.) and review weekly

The couple decided that they both would select one habit for them to work on establishing together. Kim selected weekly marriage counseling, and Rick selected date nights.

Step 1: Put Habits into Practice

To establish the first habit, they needed to find a counselor they both agreed on. In the past, Rick was reluctant to go to marriage counseling, so Kim decided to ask him about his preferences and prioritize them when searching for the right counselor. Rick didn't have many preferences, but he did share that he was hopeful that they could find a male counselor. They started by searching the internet and asking friends for recommendations. There weren't many male counselors available, but they were able to find two potential candidates. They scheduled introduction sessions to get to know each of the counselors and see if either were a good fit.

After meeting with both counselors, Rick and Kim sat down together and compared the two. One therapist was very direct; he assigned homework to clients and had a very particular way in which the couple would go through the counseling process. The other counselor was more flexible, had a process that was dictated by the couple, and offered virtual counseling that they could attend from home. They both decided to go with the more flexible counselor and felt good about his potential to help them.

Next, they had to figure out a good day and time they could consistently schedule their weekly counseling appointments without distractions. They settled on Wednesdays at 6:00 p.m., as Kim's mom stated she would be supportive and watch the baby during that time every week. They would both also be done with work by 4:00 p.m. every Wednesday, giving them enough time to get home, eat, and be mentally ready for their counseling session. To establish the date night habit, they needed to first decide what day of the week would be best. Given that they don't work on Saturdays or Sundays, they chose Saturday so they could enjoy the evenings, and possibly nights, together if they decided. Saturdays were more difficult to plan, though, as they didn't have childcare due to their parents' inconsistent availability on the weekends. To address this obstacle, they decided to explore flexible childcare options they could use on a regular basis.

They went to an online childcare website and created an account. They then did some research on potential sitters who were available, affordable, and highly rated for working with younger kids. They found three individuals they felt may be a good fit, and over the next two weeks, they scheduled interviews with each potential candidate.

After the interviews were concluded, they discussed the candidates and chose the individual they felt best about. To increase their comfortability, they asked if this individual could come and watch their child while they were present so they could assess the sitter's ability and their child's comfort level. They also purchased two nanny cams so they could easily check in on their son when they were out. After observing the sitter, they felt comfortable moving forward with establishing the habit.

Step 2: Assess Consistency of Habits

The couple decided to check in on their goals after 60 days. This gave them a total of eight counseling sessions to attend. At the 60-day mark, they were able to see they attended seven of the eight scheduled counseling sessions. There was one Wednesday when Kim's mother was unable to babysit, so they had to cancel their counseling session, and they were unable to reschedule it due to their busy schedules. It should be noted that they have attended six consecutive sessions and feel that, overall, this habit has been consistent.

Regarding the assessment of their consistency of observing date nights—they had four potential Saturdays for date nights over the last 60 days. However, they were able to attend only two. One of the date nights was canceled due to the baby not feeling well and Kim not being comfortable leaving the baby with a sitter during that time. Another date night had to be canceled due to the sitter not being available on

Mastering Your Process

that Saturday. Since they've only gone on 50% of the scheduled date nights, this habit has not been consistent at this point.

Step 3: Assess Pros and Cons of Habits

Next, the couple was tasked with assessing the pros and cons of each habit. Due to the inconsistency of the date nights, they could not accurately assess the pros and cons of that habit. So, they just focused on assessing the pros and cons of weekly marriage counseling.

Marriage Counseling Habit Pros:

- Consistently discussing conflicts and avoiding building tension
- Mediator helping both to feel heard
- Both improving listening skills
- Better understanding between the couple
- Improved intimacy and connection
- Less individual stress in other areas of their lives

Marriage Counseling Habit Cons:

- Weekly $30 copay for each session
- Some sessions have been emotionally painful
- Some concerns about being too dependent on counseling to fix issues

Step 4: Continue or Adjust/Stop Habits

After assessing each habit, the couple must decide if the habits are worth continuing or if they need to adjust or completely discontinue them. The couple decided to discuss the habits in their most recent counseling session to have a mediator assist them in evaluating the best course of action moving forward.

Kim expressed a strong preference to continue marriage counseling and pointed out how important the benefits have been in their marriage. Rick expressed some reluctance and shared that he figured once things were fixed, he would no longer need to attend marriage counseling. When reviewing the benefits, he did share that he understands how much they have improved and how much more work they must do, so he agreed that continuing counseling was more beneficial than not. Rick highlighted that due to marital counseling, he noticed improvements in other areas of his life that are not directly related to his marriage.

One example was his ability to tolerate and cope with the stressors of teaching at a university. He shared that he didn't notice how irritable he was at work until he felt his mood and marriage improve. He noticed that other areas of his life continue to get better as his marriage gets better. He stated that this was one of the extra benefits that motivated him to continue to improve their relationship.

Due to the inconsistency of date nights, they were unable to accurately assess the pros or cons of that habit. Both noted that on the two date nights that they did have, they enjoyed connecting with each other without the baby. The first date night they went on was the first they had scheduled in over six months. They both shared that they hadn't noticed how long it had been and admitted it was something that hadn't been at the forefront of their minds. They agreed that this was something they should continue so they could have scheduled time to focus on one another.

When reviewing the obstacles that got in their way, they highlighted the importance of having backup measures in place for when things didn't go according to schedule—like the sitter not being able to watch the baby on a date night weekend. To account for those types of situations, they discussed having other sitters to fall back on and decided to go through the hiring process again so they could have more than one babysitter to use. This way, if one sitter was ever unavailable, they could follow up with the second option. They could use this same strategy if Kim's mom was ever unable to watch the baby during a marriage counseling session.

They also discussed using sitters more often for things like wanting a break and needing time to grade papers or work on research projects. Having more sitters available would help them prioritize their self-care and establish more consistency for date nights. They also decided that if neither babysitter were available for a date night, they would ask one of their parents. Although their parents aren't *always* available on weekends, they may be able to help if both sitters are unavailable.

As far as the baby being sick, an extra sitter wouldn't solve that issue. Since date night is something that is scheduled every other week, that means there is a week

Mastering Your Process

in which there is no scheduled date night. So, they decided if a date were missed due to the baby or one of them being sick, that they would try to reschedule it during a non-date night weekend.

This would give them back-to-back date nights, but it would help them be consistent in having date nights at least twice a month. Using these strategies will help them increase the consistency of date nights and properly assess the pros and cons of practicing this habit.

Step 5: Continue/Add Habits and repeat

Now the couple must work together and decide to continue focusing on the same habits or revisit the list and add new habits if they feel the old ones are well-established.

Marriage Counseling Habit:

Do we complete the desired behavior consistently? **Yes.**

Do we complete the behavior unconsciously? **Yes.**

Does the behavior require little effort in comparison to when we first established it? **No, Rick and Kim both shared that therapy continues to require a lot of effort and emotional energy. Rick shared there are times he does not want to go and must remind himself of the overall benefits.**

The marriage counseling habit has made progress and continues to be successful, but according to the couple, it is not an established habit yet. Although it is consistent, it is still requiring focused effort. They will focus on this habit, follow the steps in the cycle, and re-assess it in another 60 days.

Date Night Habit:

Do we complete the desired behavior consistently? **No.**

Do we complete the behavior unconsciously? **No.**

Does practicing the behavior require less effort than it did when I first established it? **No.**

Mastering Your Process

The date night habit has not been well-established at this point. The couple was able to evaluate the obstacles in their way and develop several strategies to address them. They will put the strategies into place and continue to focus on establishing this habit.

***

Now you have been able to see three examples in which a process-driven mindset was used to achieve desired outcomes and dreams. Try not to get too caught up in the different habits that each example was focused on. These may not be habits that lead you to similar desired outcomes, and that is okay. What's important is to follow the outlined steps to see what will best benefit you and then take action. The process is the most important principle to take from the examples—not the outcomes or what's important to the individuals in the examples. We all have different values, and that should be used to determine what you want to focus on and how you achieve success. Now that you have seen some examples, we will use the next chapter to outline your personal steps to achieve your own desired outcomes.

CHAPTER 7 KEY POINTS:

- Step 1: Put Habits into Practice

    o   Start taking steps to establish your habits

- Step 2: Assess Consistency of Habits

    o   Review if you are consistently doing what you set out to do

- Step 3: Assess Pros and Cons of Habits

    o   Take an honest look at the pros and cons of your new actions

- Step 4: Continue or Adjust/Stop Habits

    o   Decide if you should keep the new habits, adjust them, or stop them completely

- Step 5: Continue/Add Habits and Repeat

    o   If your new habits are well-established, you can now add more to focus on

CHAPTER 8: ESTABLISHING YOUR PROCESS (ACTION PLAN)

This chapter will provide a guide to assist you in the beginning stages of mastering your process. Use the template included to focus on a specific outcome-driven goal or dream of yours that is important to you. Be sure to take your time; this journey requires patience.

If you are highly motivated, this can be difficult, but rushing can hinder the goal of focusing on establishing habits instead of focusing on the desired outcomes. Remember, establishing habits can take time, but they render great results over a lifespan.

Desired Outcomes/Dreams

First, you must list your desired outcomes and dreams. You can be as detailed or as general as you like. Think specifically about what changes you want to see in your life. This can be better health, better finances, some improved ability, or anything else that's important to you. Be sure to think very critically about what is the most important, and list them in the space below:

_____

_____

_____

_____

_____

_____

_____

Motivations/Reasons

Now that you have your dreams listed, you must list your motivations and/or reasons for wanting them. Listing as many as possible now can aid you during the rest of the process if you face obstacles that discourage you.

_____

_____

_____

_____

_____

_____

Mastering Your Process
<u>Exploring Habits</u>

Now you must decide where you will get information on the necessary habits to increase the likelihood of the outcomes that you desire. Do not rush this process. You may have an idea of the habits needed, but it can never hurt to research and consider things you may be missing. List whom you will talk to about this (specific friends, coworkers, mentors, parents, etc.). Also, list any resources you may look to for information, such as webinars, trainings, websites, books, etc.

- _____
- _____
- _____
- _____
- _____
- _____
- _____
- _____
- _____
- _____
- _____

Habits to Establish

Once you have taken the time to explore the habits necessary for your desired outcomes, you are ready to list them. This list can be as long or as short as you need it to be. Do not be afraid to list many habits, as you will have time to narrow your focus to just a few. You can also add more habits later if you learn of new ones that are necessary for you to reach your dreams.

Once you have your list, circle up to three that you want to focus on. Consider what habits will be easiest to establish because they'll create momentum and a sense of success, leading you to be even more motivated for the more difficult habits.

- _____
- _____
- _____
- _____
- _____
- _____
- _____
- _____
- _____

Mastering Your Process
Step 1: Put Habits into Practice

Now it's time to initiate your process-driven cycle. Make sure you have everything in place to support your habit. Set reminders on your phone calendar, share your goals with those who support you, and adjust your schedule as needed. Get anything that may be helpful to complete your habit. This could be workout clothes and a gym membership or a new bank account and a money-saving application for your phone. Outline any steps you must take before beginning your habit below. As you complete the steps, cross them off. Once they are all completed, you can begin establishing your new habit. If you are focusing on more than one habit, follow these instructions for each of them.

- Steps: _____
  _____

- Steps: _____
  _____

- Steps: _____
  _____

- Steps: _____
  _____

- Steps: _____
  _____

Step 2: Assess Consistency of Habits

Before moving forward with establishing your habit, set a check-in date to assess its consistency. It is encouraged to assess your habit every 30-60 days in the beginning.

Once you select a date, list the desired frequency in which you should observe the habit. Is this something you should do daily, twice a week, biweekly, monthly, or something else? For example, if the habit is to work out three days a week, and you plan to check in every eight weeks, the desired frequency would be 24 days of working out. That is 3 days a week × 8 weeks.

Once you have the check-in day and the desired frequency, you can assess if this habit is consistent by dividing the desired frequency by the actual number of days you completed the habit and multiplying that number by 100. This will give you the percentage of how often you practiced the habit. A good rule of thumb is to score 75% or higher to deem the habit consistent.

For each habit, list the check in-date and desired frequency. Underneath the check-in date, enter the number of days the habit was completed and calculate the frequency. Do this for all habits you are currently focusing on.

If your habit is deemed inconsistent, you must address any obstacles that affect your consistency before moving to the next step. Don't be afraid to seek help at this stage. Sometimes, just processing your issues with someone you trust can clear your mind and help you decide what strategies to use. Other times, it can give you the opportunity to receive helpful advice.

- HabitCheck-InDate:_____
    o Desired Frequency of Habit: _____
    o Number of Days Habit Completed: _____
    o Consistency of Habit (Number of Days Habit Completed divided by Desired Frequency × 100): _____

Example:

Andre is focusing on establishing a habit of attending weekly counseling for his depression. He plans to assess his habit in eight weeks to see if he is consistently practicing it. Over an eight-week period, he would have the desired frequency of eight therapy sessions.

Andre attends four out of his eight scheduled therapy sessions. His check-in information is provided below.

Christopher Robinson

- Habit Check-In Date: January 1, 2023 (60 days)
    - o Desired Frequency of Habit: **8**
    - o Number of Days Habit Completed: **4**
    - o Consistency of Habit (Number of Days Habit Completed divided by Desired Frequency × 100): **(4÷8) × 100 = 50%**

Andre has completed the habit only 50% of the time. Due to it not being at least 75%, it is deemed inconsistent. He now has to troubleshoot problems before moving to the next step.

Step 3: Assess Pros and Cons of Habits

Remember, you cannot accurately complete this step for a habit without consistently putting that habit into action. Once your habit has been consistent for at least 30-60 days, you can list its pros and cons. This can be difficult, as there are usually multiple things that impact pros and cons.

Your habit may not be the sole reason for a pro or a con, so try to only list things that you've noticed since establishing the habit and things that you can easily link to the new habit. For example, if you have been consistently exercising and now you notice less aches in your back, exercise is likely the reason for

Mastering Your Process

your back relief. Sure, eating healthier, change in the weather, and less stress could contribute to this relief, but it's also a direct result of exercising, so you should list it under the pros. List as many pros and cons as you can think of. If you have multiple habits you're focusing on, repeat this step for each of them.

Pros

- _____
  _____

- _____
  _____

- _____
  _____

- _____
  _____

- _____
  _____

- _____
  _____

- _____
  _____

Cons

- _____
  _____

- _____
  _____
  _____

- _____
  _____
  _____

- _____
  _____
  _____

- _____
  _____
  _____

- _____
  _____
  _____

- _____
  _____

Step 4: Continue or Adjust/Stop Habits

At this point, you have three options to consider for your habit(s). It's time to decide if you should keep the new habit(s), adjust them, or stop them completely. This is a personal choice, but it's extremely important to consider several aspects. Some

Mastering Your Process

habits may be easy to continue, as the pros obviously outweigh the cons. However, when the pros and cons are more balanced, it can make the decision more difficult. Answer the following questions to help you make your decision.

Does the new habit improve my overall well-being?

_____
_____
_____

What is the worst that can happen if I keep this habit in place?

_____
_____
_____

What is the best thing that can happen if I keep this habit in place?

_____
_____
_____

Is the overall cost of the habit worth the current benefits?

_____

_____

_____

Is there a way for me to adjust the habit to decrease any risk or cost without sacrificing too many of the benefits?

_____

_____

_____

Being honest when answering these questions will help you make the decision that is best for you, so remember the importance of being honest with yourself. If you disregard potential risk, you could find yourself with an unintended consequence. Recall the Bernie Madoff example and what his habits cost him.

Step 5: Continue/Add Habits and Repeat

At the final step of the cycle, you must answer the questions below and decide if the habits you have chosen to continue are well-established. If the answer is "yes" to all three questions,

Mastering Your Process

you can consider that habit "well-established" and add another habit from your original list to focus on. Answer the questions below for each habit you are currently working to establish.

Do I complete the desired behavior on a consistent basis?

_____

_____

Do I complete the behavior unconsciously?

_____

_____

Does practicing the behavior require less effort than it did when I first established it?

_____

_____

***

Now that you have your action plan, you want to make sure it's something that you see often. Visualization helps keep things at the forefront of your mind while you go about your day. This is extremely important for those who are busy. Imagine a parent who has to take care of their kids, clean their house, cook, and make sure they fulfill all the obligations of their career. It would be very easy for them to have great intentions with their goals but get lost in their regular daily duties.

It can be difficult to implement new habits even when they're important to us. Having regular reminders on why you started this journey in the first place can help keep you on track, especially in the beginning.

So, is this action plan something that you'll make copies of and hang up in your bathroom? Or is this something that you'll keep a digital copy of on your computer at work? Or maybe it's something you write down and put on the front of your school binder. The choice is yours, so decide how you want to look at your action plan on a regular basis. This doesn't mean that you must spend time reading through it every single day—just seeing it will serve as a reminder of what you're focusing on.

CHAPTER 8 KEY POINTS:

- Ensure you're patient on this journey of establishing new habits.

- Take time to effectively explore the habits you need for the dreams you have.

- Start with the habits that appear easy before attempting the more difficult ones.

- Seek help when you run into obstacles.

CHAPTER 9: CONCLUSION

At this point, you have hopefully begun to focus on your process. It is my assumption that most of you who picked up this book have an idea of the dreams and outcomes that you want to achieve. The thing that usually gets people stuck is focusing on *how* they're going to do that. There are always many ways to get things done, but there is usually a best way. To figure out the best way, you must evaluate the pros and cons along your journey. When this is not given enough attention, it increases the likelihood of you missing out on potential advantages and disadvantages.

In essence, this is the ability to watch what you're doing and recognize the impact of your actions. When you develop the capacity to do this on a regular basis, you begin to maximize your potential while also avoiding major pitfalls that you would otherwise miss. Sure, there are a lot of benefits to being extremely focused and keeping your eye on the prize, but this can also lead to you tripping along the way or missing out on other prizes due to being hyper-focused on what lies ahead.

Mastering Your Process

Mastering your process is about being efficient while also avoiding undervaluing your dreams. When you have very specific goals, you are pressured to make realistic deadlines and expectations. This is not all bad, as it helps us stay on track…but what if you're aiming too low?

If you're running toward a finish line, there's also a chance that once you get to it, all your energy will leave your body. You see it all the time when sprinters finish a race. And when you think about it, it's similar to losing all motivation once you achieve a goal.

So, you must ask yourself what it is that you really want on your journey. Is it to earn a certain amount of money or to maximize your earning potential? Is it to reach a certain weight or to be as healthy as possible? Do you want to get married, or do you want to have a joyous and harmonious relationship with a partner? Focusing on maximizing your potential on your journey does not exclude these specific outcomes that you may want. In fact, if you focus more on the journey and maximizing your potential, the outcomes that you want will likely happen as a result. You will most likely even get additional benefits due to you not losing motivation or focusing on just one specific outcome.

The person who wants to maximize their earning potential will likely earn the amount of money that they originally wanted to. The person who wants a joyous and harmonious relationship will likely get married. And the individual who strives to be as healthy as possible will reach the weight that they initially wanted.

Becoming process-driven does not push your outcomes and dreams to the side—it increases the likelihood of you achieving them *and* gaining more. Continue to focus on establishing habits and not so much on trying to reach a certain outcome. This will help you notice an impact in multiple areas of your life if you're honest in your assessment of the pros and cons along your journey.

Be blessed and, most importantly, be patient with yourself, as the work that you're getting ready to embark on is no small feat… but it will lead to great rewards.

Mastering Your Process

ACKNOWLEDGMENTS

Authoring a book has been a difficult, yet an enlightening task. I know this would not have been possible without the life lessons I've been blessed with. With that in mind, I must specifically thank my mother Lesa Forrest, my father Andre Robinson, and my stepfather Douglas Forrest. Every professional endeavor I have embarked on, you all have been nothing but supportive. Even as an adult, you all continue to be my biggest cheerleaders, motivating me to maximize my potential. For that, I will be forever grateful.